First Facts

The Solar System

# Working in Space

by Steve Kortenkamp

**Consultant:**
James Gerard
Aerospace Education Specialist, NASA
Kennedy Space Center, Florida

Capstone
press

Mankato, Minnesota

First Facts is published by Capstone Press,
151 Good Counsel Drive, P.O. Box 669, Mankato, Minnesota 56002.
www.capstonepress.com

*Library of Congress Cataloging-in-Publication Data*
Kortenkamp, Steve.
  Working in space / by Steve Kortenkamp.
    p. cm. — (First facts. The solar system)
  Summary: "Describes the training and duties of astronauts who work in space shuttles and
space stations" — Provided by publisher.
  Includes bibliographical references and index.
  ISBN–13: 978–1–4296–1261–6 (hardcover)
  ISBN–10: 1–4296–1261–4 (hardcover)
  1.  Manned space flight — Juvenile literature. 2.  Space flight — Physiological effect —
Juvenile literature. 3.  Astronauts — Job descriptions — Juvenile literature.  I. Title. II. Series.
TL793.K6633 2008
629.45 — dc22                                                                    2007023034

**Editorial Credits**
Lori Shores and Christopher L. Harbo, editors; Juliette Peters, set designer; Kim Brown, book
    designer and illustrator; Linda Clavel, photo researcher

**Photo Credits**
NASA, 1, 5, 6, 7, 8, 10, 13, 14, 17, 18, 19, 20, 21, cover
Photodisc, back cover
Wikipedia, public-domain image/NASA, 11

1 2 3 4 5 6 13 12 11 10 09 08

# Table of Contents

# Zero Gravity

Floating in space sure looks fun. Astronauts float because it feels like there isn't any **gravity**. But working in zero gravity is much harder than it looks. Astronauts train for years before they are ready to work in space.

# Astronaut Training

Astronauts train for about 10 years before working in space. They fly in jets that make steep dives. During the dives, astronauts practice working in **weightlessness**.

Astronauts also train underwater to practice moving equipment. Astronauts and their equipment float underwater, just like in space.

## Space Walks and Suits

Astronauts wear space suits when they go on **space walks**. There's no air in space. It gets very hot in the sunlight and very cold in the shade. Space suits give astronauts air to breathe. The suits also protect them from hot and cold temperatures.

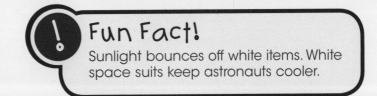

**Fun Fact!**
Sunlight bounces off white items. White space suits keep astronauts cooler.

# Building a Space Station

The United States, Russia, and other countries are working together to build the *International Space Station*. Astronauts live and work at the space station.

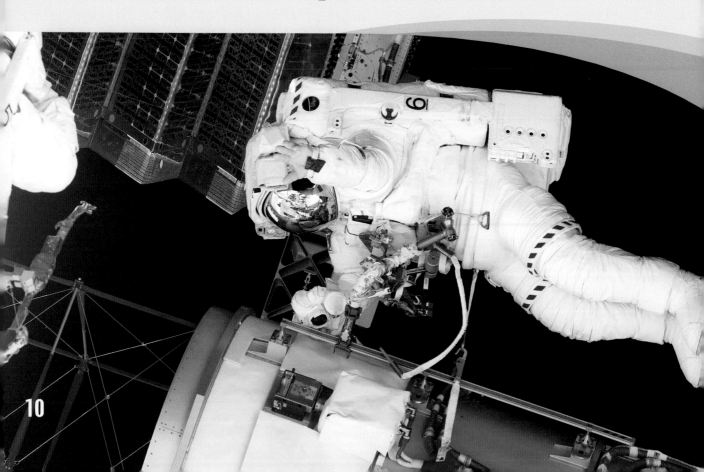

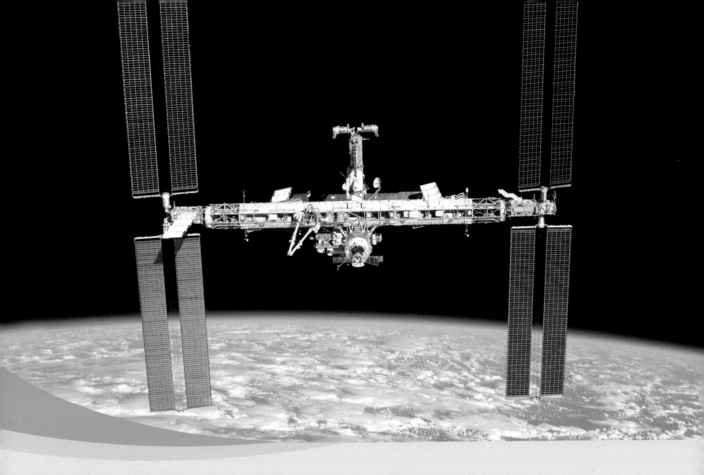

The space station will be taller than a 10 story building when finished. Space shuttles carry new pieces of the station into space. It will take 45 trips to get all the pieces up to the space station.

# Astronaut Tools

Astronauts use special tools to build the space station. One tool is a giant robot arm attached to the station. Astronauts use the robot arm to pull new pieces out of the space shuttle. Then they bolt the pieces to the station during space walks.

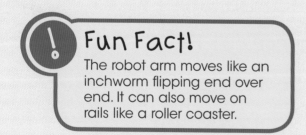

**Fun Fact!**

The robot arm moves like an inchworm flipping end over end. It can also move on rails like a roller coaster.

robot arm

13

## Science Experiments

Astronauts also work on **experiments** in space. They study how living in space changes the body. They've learned that weightlessness weakens a person's bones and muscles.

Astronauts also study how fire acts in space. It spreads out like a ball. The experiments help scientists make better space station smoke detectors.

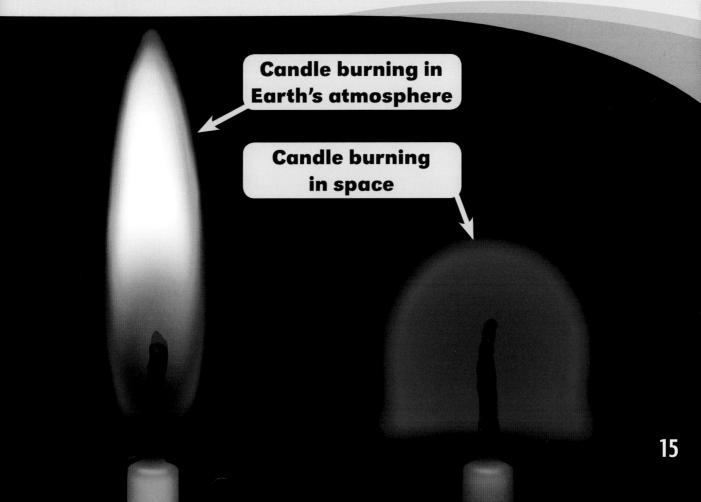

Candle burning in Earth's atmosphere

Candle burning in space

# Time for Play

Astronauts work hard but they still have free time. They read books, listen to music, and toss around soccer balls.

In 2007, astronaut Sunita Williams ran the Boston **Marathon**. But she wasn't in Boston. She ran the marathon on the space station's treadmill!

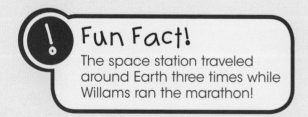

**Fun Fact!**
The space station traveled around Earth three times while Willams ran the marathon!

# Robot Helpers

Working in space sometimes means staying on Earth. Scientists use **space probes** to study planets and other objects in space. Robots sometimes return material to Earth for scientists to study.

Someday robots may also help astronauts in space. These robots will warn astronauts of dangers on the space station.

# Amazing but True!

Astronauts working on the space station live in space for a long time. They celebrate birthdays, anniversaries, and holidays in space. Most astronauts stay for at least six months. The longest any person has stayed in space is one year, two months, and ten days.

# Think Big!

Astronauts have worked on many types of spacecraft, including space shuttles and the space station. Some astronauts have even worked on the Moon. Today, astronauts are studying ways to work on Mars. If you were an astronaut, where would you want to work?

# Glossary

**experiment** (ek-SPER-uh-ment) — a scientific test to find out how something works

**gravity** (GRAV-uh-tee) — a force that pulls objects together

**marathon** (MAR-uh-thon) — a race that covers 26 miles, 385 yards (about 42 kilometers)

**space probe** (SPAYSS PROHB) — a spacecraft that travels to other planets and outer space

**space walk** (SPAYSS WAWK) — a period of time during which an astronaut leaves the spacecraft to move around in space

**weightlessness** (WATE-liss-ness) — a state in which a person feels free of the pull of Earth's gravity

# Read More

**Bredeson, Carmen.** *Living On a Space Shuttle.* Rookie Read-About Science. New York: Children's Press, 2003.

**Rau, Dana Meachen.** *The International Space Station.* Our Solar System. Minneapolis: Compass Point Books, 2005.

**Whitehouse, Patricia.** *Working in Space.* Space Explorer. Chicago: Heinemann, 2003.

# Internet Sites

FactHound offers a safe, fun way to find Internet sites related to this book. All of the sites on FactHound have been researched by our staff.

Here's how:
1. Visit *www.facthound.com*
2. Choose your grade level.
3. Type in this book ID **1429612614** for age-appropriate sites. You may also browse subjects by clicking on letters, or by clicking on pictures and words.
4. Click on the **Fetch It** button.

**Facthound will fetch the best sites for you!**

# Index